Noel King

SUITABLE MUSIC FOR A VIEW

SurVision Books

First published in 2024 by
SurVision Books
Dublin, Ireland
Reggio di Calabria, Italy
www.survisionmagazine.com

Copyright © Noel King, 2024

Cover image from Open Art (AI) prompt: "A surreal painting of a piano that is literally self-consuming" by SurVision Books

Design © SurVision Books, 2024

ISBN: 978-1-912963-46-1

This book is in copyright. No part of this publication may be reproduced, stored in a retrieval system, or transmitted in any form or by any means without the prior permission in writing from the publisher.

Acknowledgements

Grateful acknowledgement is made to the editors of the following, in which some of these poems, or versions of them, originally appeared:

Agenda; Bard; Boyne Berries; Can Can; Cavan Poetry Page; Census: The Fourth Seven Towers Anthology (Seven Towers, Dublin, 2014); Creature Features - The Ark of Writing (Cyprus); Drawn to the Light; Earth Love; Erbacce; First Time; Flaming Arrows; The Galway Review; The Ham; HI – Humanism Ireland; The Honest Ulsterman; Ireland of the Welcomes; Irish Medical Journal; The Journal; Kritya (India); The Lantern Review; The Linnet's Wings; The Martello; Moonstone; A New Ulster; North West Words; Orbis; Peace and Freedom; Penetang Review; Pennine Ink; Poems, Proses & Other Assorted Goodies (Malaysia); Poesis; Poets' Podium; Polestar Writers' Journal; Quantum Leap; Qutub Minar Review (India); ROPES Literary Journal; The Runt; Scrutiny2 (South Africa); Senior Times; The SHOp; Social Alternatives; Southword; Spin; Stanzas; The Stinging Fly; SurVision; Wildlife Words – Vol. 6 (Barn Owl Trust, England, 2019); Zaterdag (The Netherlands).

CONTENTS

Suitable Music for a View	7
North	8
Explosion	9
Cage	10
Funeral Days	11
Hand Me My Life	12
Earlobe	14
I Am of Titanic	15
Nocturnes	16
The Lord Save Us from All Harm	17
Monologue V	18
Jesus didn't wash his own feet	19
everybody has a swan poem, so why can't I?	20
The Cleverness of Birds	21
Women in a Kitchen	22
Plunderers	23
Chaser	24
Review	25
Mystic	26
Seeing Nothing or Where the Fuck Is Millstreet?	27
Alleyway	28
Badgers in Fenit	29
The 'Emergency'	30
The History Books	31
In Coolspark	32
The Naming of Animals	34
The Salad Boat – Gathering Leaks from the Sky	35
Hurt Her. Hurt Her. Hurt Her.	36
it is beautiful, it is, really!	37
The Watch	38
Union	39
Fire Lighting in a New Home	40

in memory of my father
Brendan King, 1930 – 2022

Suitable Music for a View

Crossing the river in Listowel
my Walkman sweeps Evita's funeral;
sounds to match a view I don't tire of
 – an odd little house by the river,
a Hollywood set of Ireland,
a scratch on the map.

North

my blackbird poem is not
singing in the dead of night
or keeping ...smooth plats of fruitful ground...
nor even feeling ...the warm eggs, the small breast...

no, my blackbird takes a break from
chirping in my west wing,
flies south
and at night east;
disturbing my sleep.

But when he goes north,
that's the thing;
when he flies north
it's serious;

catch the bugger and I am cured
but   alas   he (or she)
is invisible.

Explosion

A gas cylinder drum rolls
in and becomes the booty inside
the hideout of the young
boys on the farm by the sea.
On it they place a sheet
to hide it, graffiti its sides,
scratch the *Highly Inflammable*
words off, paint it with pirate bones.
Their families will anger for generations
about the bastards who threw the curse overboard.

Cage

Soaring into love,
two bodies become one,
fleeing respective nests
to make a new hollow.
But clipped wings can never fly again
 – in a frustrated cage
union dictating the stand.

Funeral Days

There was a time when death seemed easy;
cold, but not shivering, looking into a tomb
as a new forefather got dropped in.
There is attention to be gained in death;
Guards of Honour and reams of praise.

I want to hear poetry at my funeral.
I could chose the subject matter
or the poet, but a favourite now
could be out of vogue
by the time my time comes
– unfair to embarrass whoever's reading it.

Hand Me My Life

Your hands carry the strength
of wise old trees whose edges

of branches slapped
my childhood bedroom window.

A dumb-show plasters our faces;
a look for other drinkers in this bar,

front for our closeness, thoughts,
consolation conversations

to each others hearts.
We liken the mists of our individual

lives, lovers we have now
and one for you from the past;

likening the softness of trees
to the business of our hearts.

I condition myself to time,
make maximum use of it,

moments that take me
on epic adventures to ponder

until we next meet, when renewal
will gain fresh confidence.

My style I weave, from you my hero,
while my return is... more practical.

Now your touch is the root of it,
from hence I follow to my New World.

Earlobe

The breeze that came
      after she'd shut the door,
      after a tear came into me,
      after the first breath that upset the tears;
just brushed my earlobe.

I Am of Titanic

Did I stand calm on the deck?
How close was I to couples
like those in the film? Dammit,
I don't even know what class I travelled in.
It is preserved there for me now,

I am of Titanic.

I could know that old woman survivor
and she might know me too.
It's a kind of knowledge I welcome; no fear.

Once, the Atlantic drew me in again,
1984, just as unexpectedly
I gasped, spat, fought,
managed to survive.

I am of Titanic.

Nocturnes

*

Foghorn
figures pass each other
– shivering

*

dusk in Listowel
bring out the rats of taste
sweeping literacy

*

earth chunks chewed
by big-jawed God's
leaving mountains

The Lord Save Us from All Harm

The eleven priests came out
the morning after their reunion;
leaving thin collars in their rooms,
they stripped their black shirts off,
those that wore vests tore them from themselves.
Belts undone, they dropped their trousers,
slipped out of underpants and,
penises wobbling in the breeze,
plunged into the sea.
The waves' cold made their willies small,
snook closer to their bodies.
Seven were drowned,
four rescued, two willingly,
by the SOS that sent a boat out.

Monologue V

I have in me a need for a place
that will be everything in
dreams of escape;
a place that
no matter what
will be home,
where I will know
I do not want to come back.

Jesus didn't wash his own feet

Asking why you don't wash
your feet before going to bed,
you told me you didn't care.
All day you'd swept around
on the beach, in the caravan park,
on the dirt tracks, the sand hills,
going to the shop for ice-creams
and now, after fourteen hours of fun
you get into your nightie ready for bed with filthy feet.

I bathe mine in warm water and soap in a plastic pan
we keep under the sink. *That's just sissy,* you say
and jump into that borrowed sleeping bag without a care.

I roll the zip down on my bag and climb in,
you are on your own bunk,
start to lip a prayer, let your dark hair
fall on the day cushions with pink pillow-covers.
Soon you are snoring softly, and I dream of you
Mary Magdalene-like washing my feet,
like a good love only could, but that would be a sin
as you – lovely and all as you are – are my cousin.

In the morning we will jump into the sea
again before breakfast, paddle across the water.

everybody has a swan poem, so why can't I?

We fished and sat,
fat cats on the bank,
sharing a litre of 7up.
When I got bored
I burrowed my rod in the soft soil,
pulled out Spotlight magazine,
imagined going to hear the Horslips gig
at a place called The Stadium in Dublin.
Then you warned me about the swans,
I'd seen 'em swimmin' 'round the place,
never thought 'em any harm to be honest,
I couldn't be arsed about swans if you know what I mean,
they was just birds to me,
until you told me, you told me
they could kill a man
with them wings,
them beaks,
that the strength in 'em was amazin'.

The Cleverness of Birds

Blue tits were discovered
pecking the foil of milk bottles
so that they could drink the cream.
My grandmother swore to it
but these days we have polythene containers.

The stereotypical owl is meant to be a wise
and clever animal, but the one I got, the one
I invested in as a pet is a useless old codger,
no more a companion than a dead lion skin
on the floor in front of the fireplace.

The bird down the street talks to me, says
she hopes to go back to college next year, asks me for
a light, and what my name is. I don't tell her
and look away from her druggie eyes.
Tomorrow she can talk to someone else
here in the smoking area.

Women in a Kitchen

His wife bursts fire-lighter sticks
with rubber gloves, scatters them
on crumpled newspaper
she lights with a flick.

His mother loosens the grip
on her teacup, rearranges her cardigan,
scrapes her chair nearer the fire,
waits for the heat; still mumbling:
in my day....why in my day...
it was hard labour, no fancy contraptions
for lightin' fires.

The daughter-in-law has learned to
ignore, and 'though she feels like
poisoning the broth some days,
knows what she took on,
will be patient. Patient.

Plunderers

My bookshop...!
My books...!
Get out you bastards!
But they barge through
to their section: ripping,
plundering, angry black faces,
while we stand fear-white.
Neo Nazis push us around
into a corner, snigger and leave.
But literature stands above,
a testament to truth,
soon re-ordered, re-stocked.

Chaser

Here, let me chase this editor's lineage,
what university she studied at,
the festival's she's read from her
poetry books at, the journals her
own work has been seen in.

Then, let's look at who is
in this issue she has edited,
find the patterns that indicate
so and so also studied at such and such
a Uni; the annals that said Wendy Hope
met Robert Sisk at some festival or other.

That all the 'famous' poets had
many of their first poems published
in a small range of magazines.
Then, we will see that, yes, she is
only interested in publishing pals.

Review

He says that atoms are growing/and killing each other/in the sheds of life/that the sheds are garden ones/Is it obvious?/What is his atom?/ His metaphor?/They appear here in black on white/I can't feel any breeze when he says there is one/or hear the heart of a husband who finds a way/back through to his wife (her heart that is)/The collection is probably worth it at £9.99/But then my copy was free/I suppose it works out at about 30p a poem.

Mystic

In the poetry evening
I wait for you.

A shore sparks of rain,
sheltering among trees
that shake wet on my head;

I wait.

Seeing Nothing, or Where the Fuck Is Millstreet
For Karen O'Connor

Reading your poetry collection on the Tralee/Cork train
and after Rathmore and before Banteer, I search
rabbit-headed like through both windows,
throw reading glasses on the table, want to see all
these Rings and Raths and Fairyforts and black dogs
                       in your poems.
Your home place
of green and purple mountains,
Foxgloves and Montbretia,
Gun-barrels blazing with fir in the setting sun,
sheep and cattle cut-outs on steep gradient,
dotted sun piercing trees in the black water
and *deadly, deadly* sunshine *all* the time.
                  Childhood, your childhood *like*
as painted on your poems
but from the train I can't see nothin',
bitter, disappointed *like (and the poems seem so real)*
I wonder should this poet get a trip in the white van *like*.
There was nothin' there, I'd go for Clon or Crosseer
or Da Glen, any day, you know what I mean?
Anyway, I'm hangin' and need a wizz
but there's a fuckin' Norrie in the Jacques
and she completely missed Millstreet *like!*

  * to be delivered in a Cork accent

Alleyway

The tourist man enters
the boy's mouth,
clamps the young head
with huge hands,
rocks him to and fro,
punching his demons,
takes a while coming,

pushing luck and the devil
the boy knows'll come if he's caught.
The tourist man can
come in his mouth because
he's paying the extra dollar.
Afterwards, red faced, the tourist man
hands over the cash fast.

The child shoves the money
in a bum-bag, dons the alleyway,
buys cigarettes to take away the taste.

Badgers in Fenit
For Bridie

Your brother tells me
a badger has wandered
into your back garden,
eating all the cat food;

that after some time
has befriended your cat,
is now sharing the food.

Last night I dreamt you phoned
telling me the badgers were
"going mental" in Fenit,
that on a whim you'd poured Vodka
into the animals water dish.

On Saturday I drive out to visit you,
you're to dog-sit my golden Labrador
until Sunday week.

As my car slows down
I catch your helpless look
at your front gate,
the badger squashed dead
by the vehicle just ahead of me.

The 'Emergency'

Rationed tea, sugar, everything!
My jar   your jar   his jar
in our family of nine
all weaknesses,
sweet-tooth's showed,
every spoonful watched,
until it was empty
and the jar owner
had
to
wait
'til
next
month's rations

The History Books

Whatever happened
the book depository on Deely Plaza, Dallas,
after your man had pulled
the gun on Kennedy;
the Secret Service rushing in,
lamping him in custody
before Rudy shot him
        dead.
Whatever happened
all those school books
the children would study?
History was changed
and Lincoln became not
the only American President
shot dead,
shot dead
by the sole gunman
in the book depository room.

In Coolspark

no one cares
about yesterday,
tomorrow is not for real
except for the new releases
from Chartbusters;
our Da's give us the 2.50
and sometimes they watch with us
or we look at 'em in each other's houses
dependin' on whose parents are ou'.

Later on tonight, after the video, if I'm lucky,
Mariana, the French student will fuck me
on her host family's leather couch,
while they're at the pictures,
the Calpol-drugged kids sleepin'.

Lucky bastards, how did they get a leather couch anyway?

Last time I had it on a couch like that
your wan wiped the spunk off with a cushion for de laugh.
She didn't get to babysit there again
and blamed me, the wagon.
Mariana is a slag, but at least a bit
different to the other cunts in the estate,
the wans that whine at you for months after.
I mean, fuck it, what do they want, to be a fuckin' Da to 'em?

I hope me Da'll like this video,
keep him quiet for a while,
he likes action pictures too.
Lots of great things happen
in action pictures
and thrillers.
In Coolspark shit happens.

The Naming of Animals

There was a dog on that beach that adopted me.
We ate together an hour after meeting:
she the remains of last night's chicken,
I made a burger and chips;
I think she would have preferred the burger.

For the first month I didn't know if it was a boy
or a girl, or had a name, and didn't care
but figured I had better find out, *christen it,*
in case I had company or if I met a stranger
on the beach, I couldn't just shout *Here dog! Here dog.*

So, she was christened, or named as such;
when swimming nude in a quiet pool one evening
time, the dog paddled to the edge of the water,
her binocular eyes had me. She watched
my shriveled penis, began to pant.
I laughed, dived for my towel.

I must have been mad, because I said to the dog
that I believed in reincarnation. I, who'd had no time
for dogs (or religion) all my life. Anyway, I called her
Aphrodite. Alas, we said goodbye when I handed over
the keys of my 'muse' cottage, advising the next
occupant of the viable traits of the canine.

The Salad Boat – Gathering Leaks from the Sky

Big blue Kraft Mayonnaise buckets
placed strategically collect rainwater
in the echoing yard behind the pub.
In a random row they sit brimming
before the publican goes with his measure
and says, *I have three inches today.*

His wife having left,
sunshine hits, slips high
enough for a brief hour
to glisten in the water buckets
and a red door closes the yard
leading to the treasure trove
awaiting the publican.

Hurt Her. Hurt Her. Hurt Her.

He presses his beard into the pillow
above her shoulder, closes his eyes,

careful not to let skin-hair touch skin,
thinks of nothing but the function,

knows what she wants, a memory
of kissing her is distant. There are no groans,

just creaks in the bed. It can creak all it likes
now the last child has left home.

His heartbeat barely rises, pounding without care,
elbows not caring to support his weight like they used to.

To think of other women would be a sin, a big sin.
He wants to hurt her. Hurt her. Hurt her.

Then he showers, she purrs like a cat
sits up naked and pollutes

the bedroom with Silk Cut cigarettes.
The sight of her warped tits disgusts him.

He makes for his single bed
in the same room; sleeps quickly.

it is beautiful, it is, really!

I wish I could tell the girl opposite me
on the Piccadilly Line Tube to Heathrow
that the stunning yellow butterfly
        will not sting her,
                shit on her,
                        or harm her in any way,
that she shouldn't swat it away like a wasp or a bee;
that she should enjoy its presence so far underground
unlikely it will ever live in daylight again.
I hold up my hand,
        palm open calmly in mid-air
                in case it would like to land.
The stares I get... honest to God... the stares
                like I am some kind of psycho.

The Watch

As I placed it on the desk
little did I know
that in watching it
death was at hand.

Little did I know
that as that wrist watch sat there
the plane was already in the sky.
Little did I know
that the pilot was at suicide
and little did I know that my watch
would never be wristed
on me or anyone again
as the bomb hit.

Union

Breeze left of us, we stroll
the rock road over the cliff,
smile at the sea we've just left,
where we swam clothing-less
and kissed the salt water from our lips.
Your fingers find me,
we close hands,
your gold ring between
the crook of my 2nd and 3rd fingers;
a ring that betrotheds you to another.
Now with me in a cliff hollow
we kiss again, nibble salty tastes
from each other, nudge the flesh
of each other free.

Fire Lighting in a New Home

Who sat at this fireplace before me?
What sucks me to its ashes?
It must not stay cold,
if only for the sake of the next occupant.

Selected Poetry Titles Published by SurVision Books

Contemporary Tangential Surrealist Poetry: An Anthology
Edited by Tony Kitt
ISBN 978-1-912963-44-7

Seeds of Gravity: An Anthology of Contemporary Surrealist Poetry from Ireland
Edited by Anatoly Kudryavitsky
ISBN 978-1-912963-18-8

Invasion: An Anthology of Ukrainian Poetry about the War
Edited by Tony Kitt
ISBN 978-1-912963-32-4

Noelle Kocot. *Humanity*
(New Poetics: USA)
ISBN 978-1-9995903-0-7

Marc Vincenz. *Einstein Fledermaus*
(New Poetics: USA)
ISBN 978-1-912963-20-1

Helen Ivory. *Maps of the Abandoned City*
(New Poetics: England)
ISBN 978-1-912963-04-1

Tony Kitt. *The Magic Phlute*
(New Poetics: Ireland)
ISBN 978-1-912963-08-9

John W. Sexton. *Inverted Night*
(New Poetics: Ireland)
ISBN 978-1-912963-05-8

Afric McGlinchey. *Invisible Insane*
(New Poetics: Ireland)
ISBN 978-1-9995903-3-8

Matthew Geden. *Fruit*
(New Poetics: Ireland)
ISBN 978-1-912963-16-4

Michelle Moloney King. *Another Word for Mother*
(New Poetics: Ireland)
ISBN 978-1-912963-31-7

Tony Bailie. *Mountain Under Heaven*
(Winner of James Tate Poetry Prize 2019)
ISBN 978-1-912963-09-6

Alison Dunhill. *As Pure as Coal Dust*
(Winner of James Tate Poetry Prize 2020)
ISBN 978-1-912963-23-2

Aoife Mannix. *Alice under the Knife*
(Winner of James Tate Poetry Prize 2020)
ISBN 978-1-912963-26-3

Becki Hawkes. *The Naming of Wings*
(Winner of James Tate Poetry Prize 2021)
ISBN 978-1-912963-34-8

Ciaran O'Driscoll. *Angel Hour*
ISBN 978-1-912963-27-0

Tim Murphy. *The Mouth of Shadows*
ISBN 978-1-912963-29-4

Order our books from http://survisionmagazine.com

www.ingramcontent.com/pod-product-compliance
Lightning Source LLC
Chambersburg PA
CBHW061309040426
42444CB00010B/2563